While I'm Still Here

Howard Varney

BookLeaf Publishing

India | USA | UK

Presentation by *BookLeaf Publishing*

Web: www.bookleafpub.com

E-mail: info@bookleafpub.com

ISBN: 9789358737486

First edition 2023

To my family.

*Thank you all for being my rock, my guiding
light in my darkest days.*

ACKNOWLEDGEMENT

Thanks to BookLeaf Publishing for the #TheWriteAngle challenge. I hope I rose to it well enough to be remembered for it.

PREFACE

I have written these poems as an outlet.

At the time of writing, I am 43, divorced with no children, living alone in a small rented flat and working a "bottom-rung" job to make ends meet.

I decided to embark on the #TheWriteAngle challenge for no reason other than I had to do something rather than nothing. If you are looking for joie-de-vivre, this is the wrong book for you.

I hope that by writing these poems, I can achieve two things. If I can give just one other person in this world something to relate to, then it may have been worthwhile. And I hope the world will have a little memento to myself.

As to whether I succeed...others will be the judge of that.

Slumber

It rings. And I'll press the button.
And it'll ring again. How many this time?
You can press, but you can't win.
Rise and shine...under duress, always duress.
Only for the salary.
One more press
Though I'll rue it later.
And I'll stand and look out
Did I prep last night? What do you think?
I'll be there in time, don't worry
I have this worked out
And I'll be back later
Ready to dine, a bottle to chill
Class? Don't raise your hopes.
Glass? Don't lower your hopes
A budget brew, a grocer's pill
I'll drink to none and all, don't worry
And as it slides, then as do I
"Today in Parliament" is my aye
And midnight my no
I'll succumb soon, don't worry
For I have my routine
And a day of the same to come.

I Hope You Are Well

Good morning.
I hope you are well.
I have a computer fault.
Good morning.
I hope you are well.
Here is your renewal quote.
Good morning.
I hope you are well.
Can we re-schedule the meeting?
Good morning.
I hope you are well.
Have you planned the seating?
Good morning.
I hope you are well.
I hope you are well.
Yes, thank you, I am well.
And I'll see you in hell.
For if I weren't well
I wouldn't be working
And if I weren't well
We wouldn't be talking
And why are you asking
When you already know
You know that full well
Only too well...

Well?
And if I say "no"
What do you say then?
Do you care if I drink?
Would you just ask again?
Do you care if I cut?
Do you ask from concern?
Do you care if I cry?
Did I speak out of turn?
I won't ask how you are
Because first, I don't care
And next, you can't tell me
There's a myth you can spin
And a lie you can sell me
And I hope you are well
Like you hope I am too
Ask me tomorrow
And I'll lie anew
And you hope I am well
And I'll see you in hell
And you hope I am well
Though there's nothing to tell
And you hope I am well
And I hope I am well
But that hope will go
And I hope I am well
For that much I know
And I hope I am well
And I'll see you in hell.

Family Man

He was on Strictly just now
He did a shout-out to his partner
And to his children
And for that alone, I hate him
You did me no harm
You don't know me
You meant no ill
But yet I hate you still
I hate you not for what you do
I hate you not for what you say
I hate you not for whom you are
I hate you as that which I am not
I am 43 and loveless
I am 43 and childless
You could fail at dancing
And yet still be greater
Than I am now
And will ever be
I hate you not for what you do
Not that you even knew
I hate you not for what you say
Not that it was new today
I hate you not for whom you are
Not that you see me from afar
But loveless, childless, still I hate
Just dance and leave me to my fate.

The Councillor

The councillor sat at his desk, with admin still to
do
The clerk was in the room beside, with much a
workload too
The guard was in the foyer, with his evening
nothing new
All was calm and all was plain in chamber
number 2.

The councillor worked on his prep for Motion
number 3
With much to say and much to lose, but nothing
to decree
The clerk was busy typing, one more charge and
one more fee
The guard sat still and watched the time, with
nothing more to see.

The councillor at length stood up, his anger did
arise
A fail shall land on those who bear all burden
for his lies
The clerk clutched at his chest and gasped, his
life his only prize

And then he fell to ground and shook and slowly
closed his eyes.

"Get rid!" counselled and so the guard rose
quickly from his chair
To take away the body that was quietly lying
there
The councillor returned to work, rebuttals to
prepare
And someone else for payroll to pretend to have
a care.

And so the work continues and for most it will
be so
And some will be the whip-hand and they'll lash
more than they know
And most of us will just get far more less than
others owe
And so it all must be, until our soul is told to go.

By The Reservoir

Serene it was, still it was
Water with much to say and nothing to do
Many to see, far to walk
An oval of dark yet still colourless hue
A swift flying over, a frog jumping in
A fox somewhere wandering, starving in sin

Families visited during the day
Cars parking nearby, picnics and talk
Ramblers followed the path all around
The greater the tumult, the slower the walk
The Scouts came for hiking, the bikers to drink
Young men came for driving, the lovers to think

Nature persists and it tolerates much
It resents and laments at humanity's husk
It embraces its servants of plant and of beast
And watches the wastrels depart in the dusk
Until there is nothing of human to see
No trace of a vehicle, no wanderer to be.

Night gathers in and the water is still
The road stretches outward, no sound on its way
An owl hovers watchful, a bat frolics hopeful
Under the surface no trace of the day

Something will drink there and somewhere will
flow
Someone will learn there, but no-one will know.

Line 1 Service Desk Engineer

I sit at my desk and I am logged in
Immediate first call, cacophonous din
Answering it, now sound happy and smart
A 23K master of the art
Taking the inbound, make sure I lose none
For that's not becoming of IT Line 1
The voice is impatient, a senior director
A deal to close and they've got me to hector
Something has errored, it's urgent, get going
This is its name, the tension is growing
I mumble and click, I connect and I look
Don't recognise it, turn to the runbook
One worker per call, that's how it shall be
Won't do to overspend our client's fee
Don't know what I don't know, whom should I ask?
Someone too big to be taken to task
Frantic message typed, now I must wait
If I'm lucky he'll answer me on the same date
This is important, there's no time to lose
It's my job to fix it, not mine to accuse
The tension is growing, the voice is irate
Do I know what I'm doing? That's up for debate
I could send him higher, transfer to Line 2
But they've got more important things to do

Their task's predetermined, that's why they earn more
Who'd expect them to be on the shop floor?
Voice getting angry and I'm fully tense
I don't have an answer or even pretence
"I don't know" is no option but where can I go?
I'm bottom pay grade, so thus I must know
"Phone back when it's fixed" and so the call ends
They hung up, not me, for I must stay friends
I clutch at my face, I don't know what I don't
I could ask Line 2 but I know that they won't
So I start to document, get my call ref
Must be in the system so they can draw breath
I note down what I tried, all the regular things
They didn't fix it - and then the phone rings
So once more I answer, the same cheerful script
Always sound happy, don't let it be dipped
And so it continues, a drill for the brain
Switching from impossible to mundane
I'm counting the days here but I cannot leave
Of my poor CV I can only grieve
And I'll return home exhausted and faded
Then I get to study, my free time invaded
One must learn one's craft, it would never do
To find a caller more techie than you
And so is the pattern for those on Line 1
Helping your betters, your own honour gone.

Prayer For The Childless

As I observe the world around
I know my joy is never found
As I recall the day before
I know my soul will lift no more
As I think to the day to come
I know my heart is turning numb
God guide me now, God guide me on
I ask for light and ways to learn
God guide me now, God lead again
And tell me how my life may turn

My line is ending with my soul
My life is now devoid of goal
My sons and daughters are no more
And thus my soul has gone to war
I lift my face up to the sky
To do, to be, I must ask why
God guide me now, God guide me on
And let me find my purpose now
God guide me now, God lead again
As much as love and joy allow

Macclesfield

Cheshire's unruly terrier
A Peak District gatekeeper
Standing on its own
Yet in the shadow of its wealthy siblings
And never knowing its place
North, a grimy emperor
South, a gurning baron
East, a quiet lieutenant
West, an ageing lord
Let us ascend the 108
And mourn the Majestic
Then where the canal may take us
We'll go and drink with Maggoty
Let West Coast bring us something
For we have nowhere to gamble
Culture indeed, is it a thing?
A place at least to ramble
Fans congregate on Saturday
For United and City are calling
Liverpool is leftfield
And the Silkmen know their place
Ian is looking down on us
He had the right idea
We'll yearn for better times that were
And we'll sit idly now.

Culture War

"If you like Them, then leave my Friends list."
"If you support Them, then leave my Friends
list."
And it's that simple, is it?
You know Them all, do you?
You know more than me, do you?
You're without fault, are you?
You've seen inside my head, have you?
You're the arbiter, are you?
It's a free country, isn't it?
I'm not one of Them now, but I was
I know what I stand for
I know what I stood for
I may not stand by what I stood by
But I know whose body I stood in
You don't know that like I did
And do you trust me to think?
To lose you as a friend makes me sad
But I do not leave you
It is you who leaves me
You who do not trust me
And who presumes to judge me
Surround yourself, if you will
By what you want to hear
You're less than you believe

Your name does not precede you
Bygones can be bygones
But only when you're ready
And when you choose to trust me
I'll be ready
Send Request again, Accept again
Converse again
Yes, I'll be ready.

The Absurd Mr Collins

A bright and sunny morning
Broke out over St Eves
A day to warm the heart and soul
Of any who believes

Collins was in the kitchen
Good coffee in the pot
Sweetened with two sugars
And blown for being too hot

He glanced at phone and paper
With little to detect
Then drank the dregs and stepped outside
A journey to select

He walked towards the junction
But as he did so heard
The laughter of a little boy
Whose mirth he had incurred.

"Daft shirt!" the boy said, laughing
Collins shrugged and turned
"Your time," he said, and strolled on
The boy's attention spurned

As he continued walking
At length he touched his palm
Then made a silent gesture
Demeanour staying calm

He walked into a public park
And strolled around the gardens
He listened to the birdsong
Then bade a dozen pardons

To whom it was, for whom it was
No indication spoken
Yet birds sang loud and louder still
A consciousness awoken

Collins turned and traced his steps
Striding for his home
He passed the local churchyard
Sun gleaming from the dome

Collins walked along the road
The other side he heard
The screams of pain and sorrow
He tutted "How absurd".

A crowd gathered the other side
A body on the ground
A little boy, once flush with life
No longer made a sound

Collins opened his front door
And let it close behind
A silence passed within the walls
No answer there to find

A whole day passed and one again
A stillness through the town
Yet days will dawn and times will be
Until the sun goes down.

May I Grieve?

I am a man with no cause to complain
Better off than many
But may I grieve?
Privileged in most ways you can mention
White, male, straight, cis
Lazy as hell but still able-bodied
Introspective as hell but still able-minded
But may I grieve?
OK, maybe not privileged in the wealth sense
Not that it's for want of trying though
I have a family who love me
And a roof over my head
I can put food on my table
And step outside whenever I choose
But may I grieve?
I can put want I want on TV
Get up when I want at the weekend
Listen to what I want on the radio
Watch what I want on my phone
But may I grieve?
I wake up in my bed alone
A dick that doesn't function
I'm not firing blanks, you see
I've got live rounds but no gun
So may I grieve?

I've never known
The pain of losing a child
I can't presume
I've mourned nobody younger
But may I grieve?
You can't lose what you don't have
So may I grieve?
Some mourn for that which was
I mourn for that which never was
And likely never will be
So may I grieve?
Ought I to grieve?
What right have I to grieve?
How selfish of me to grieve
How lucky I am
To get up when I like
And do what I like
Subject to the constraints of a low salary
Living in a place that's not mine
That may be taken away again
So may I grieve?
Many think their best days are behind them
As do I, indeed, as do I
From happily married in years past
To living alone in years present
So may I grieve?
Living to work to lament
So may I grieve?
"Middle age is a great time of your life"

Say successful celebrities with children
So may I grieve?
Do I deserve to grieve?
Have I had my time to grieve?
Who am I to grieve?
Who am I at all?
If I'm not worth anything
Then I'm worth this question
If I'm worth this question
Then I'm worth an answer
And so I'll ask again:
Please...
May I grieve?

Fantasies

I turned on the radio, it was Radio 3
Not a frequent choice, if you know me
Pianist played Ravel, very impressive
A skill appreciated by this depressive
Footballer, pop star, I'd wanted it all
When I was singing hymns in assembly hall
They make it look easy, more's the pity
Turning you into real-life Walter Mitty
I couldn't kick a ball more than 10 feet
I wasn't going to get signed by Chester-le-Street
But piano was my thing, back in the day
Performance diploma before my first lay
Then graduate finance became my ambition
Chasing the money, to hell with perdition
It never happened, my career just slid
And I'm left regretting the subjects I did
A small Yamaha keyboard sits in my flat
Gathering dust, no less value for that
I still cling to hopes that I'll plonk out a song
Hoping to salvage a career gone wrong
One play on 6 Music, or Radio 2
Hell, at this point Radio Derby would do
A poundstretcher Billy Joel, I'd settle for
If I never had to pay rent or mortgage any more
But who am I kidding? What fool am I?

The hope of fame remains the permanent lie
And I'll disappear, though most never saw me
And all that I'll cling to is others before me.

Prayer For The Lonely

If I should see you drink alone
And I should see your tears
I pray for strength and grace of mind
To trust you as my peers
If I should see you walk alone
With no-one else to stand
I pray that I will speak the truth
While holding out my hand
If I should see you on the edge
And waiting for the fall
I pray that I may give to you
A cause to hear life's call
If I should think only of me
And turn my face away
I pray that wisdom will return
And we will share the day.

Buxton

A stonemason's jewel
Swallowed by a national park
Inside the Peak District
On everything but the map
Near to beauty, near to brains
And yet far from vigour
A goose and a train
Pay homage to a park
And a Saturday visitor
Let's see the actors
Let's see the artisans
And then we'll go away again
Some don't need to worry
For the city's far enough away
And some are terrified
For the city's far enough away
I'll trade you a moorhen
For one student rock band
Then we'll go and drink water
And drift by the Crescent
We'll pretend we're in Vegas
Then come to our senses
We'll all grow old gracefully
The Peak District's patrol.

Drinking

With a glass of white wine
I'll drink, then drink to you
With a glass of red wine
I'll salute all that you do
With a tall vodka-orange
I'll greet all on the Earth
With a shallow Cointreau
I'll cheer all that I'm worth
With a cool pint of beer
I'll give heart to your sorrow
With a cold cloudy cider
I'll be wishing your tomorrow
With an iced single malt
I'll bow down to the nation
With a glass of spiced rum
I'll give you my invitation
With a short glass of gin
I'll bequeath all my greeting
With a round glass of brandy
To humankind's meeting
I'll drink now and talk now
I hope the world knows it
I thank you for goodwill
And hope no-one forgoes it.

Just A Number

We congratulate those
Who have just had a baby
Yes, good for them.
Does that also mean
We commiserate those
Who have no children
Like we commiserate those
Who fail an exam?
You can't prove a negative
You can't react
To what doesn't happen.
We say "Get Well Soon"
To the injured
We send cards and flowers
And what of the disabled?
If it never changes
Then what's there to notice?
They say age is just a number
It doesn't matter
How old you are
And you know what?
So's my blood pressure.
So's my sperm count.
So's the speed limit.
So's the number of eggs left

In a woman's ovaries.
So's your salary.
So's your overdraft.
So's the minutes you were waiting
For that appointment
Who never showed up.
So's the average age
Of a professional athlete.
Or pilot. Or soldier.
All just numbers, right?
Don't patronise me
It's more than a number
It's a definer
Let's meet today's contestants:
"Hello, I'm David
38 from Swindon
And I'm a civil engineer."
"Hello, I'm Catherine
66 from Glasgow
And I'm a retired teacher."
"Hello, I'm Joanne
31 from Bristol
And I'm a doctor."
"Hello, I'm Barry
Blood group O Negative from Kent
And I'm a drain on the economy."
Is what you won't hear.
And we'll all go on
Saying what others want to hear

And we'll all go on
Not acknowledging that
Which makes us feel bad
And we'll all go on
In denial again
And a number's a number
Its value is everything.

Flying

As I'm flying, let me see the land
The green and brown, Nature's command
I'll glide, I'm free, I greet the air
I kiss the breeze, I feel it there
I'm on a path that has no end
The Earth, this sphere will be my friend
Plant, fish, beast, all down below
And where they lead, we cannot know
I journey still, the air is clear
No enemy is waiting here
So let me fly and let me sing
And find what Nature yet may bring
For now this path gives joy anew
And all I learn, I wish to you.

Skylands Bridge

A September evening, the air is fresh
Cool on the face, to tingle flesh
The Skylands River shimmers its way
Red sky above, below red clay
Across the river the brickwork ridge
And angry metal of Skylands Bridge
Across the bridge the traffic thunders
The miles to eat and petrol plunders
The town admires its industry
From smelted metal to felling tree.

Cars and trucks all past their prime
And walkers cross from time to time
All take the bridge and most will gaze
To see the river's shimmering haze
Time slides on, the sky grows darker
The night time shall put down its marker
The traffic thins, disperses, drifts
From labour's exodus to social lifts
Then as a starlit sky takes hold
A man emerges in the cold.

Nondescript describes him best
Middle years, scarred from time's test
In his hands he holds a ladder

On his face the wrinkles sadder
His shoulders bear a large backpack
A walker's friend, a labourer's rack
He stops upon the bridge's centre
Time is past for traffic to enter
Into the backpack now he'll paw
Thick rope and whisky to withdraw.

The morning dawns, the bridge is closed
The traffic waits at ends opposed
From the bridge a body hangs
Police plus ambulance harangues
The body leaves under a sheet
Hats removed, a kin to meet
Abandoned ladder with empty bottle
A rope cut free from victim's throttle
All are taken, none are left
And traffic resumes, knowledge bereft.

Ah, Skylands Bridge, what you have seen
A life that has no longer been
In days to come, there will be those
Who'll honour one that no-one knows
Some flowers left, a message scrawled
Prayers left for a soul recalled
Some will gossip as they're walking
Nothing seen yet memories stalking
And vehicles charge as water plays
A town at work, society strays.

One Day

I tell myself it'll happen.
One day.
I'll be validated.
One day.
I won't have to count the days.
One day.
I'll be a lover.
One day.
I'll be a father.
One day.
I'll have a valued profession.
One day.
My parents made me
Just as their parents made them
And their parents made them
And we go back, back back
To the time before we crawled out of the water
Am I to be
The end of that line?
Does my DNA stop
Like a tramway terminus?
Will all those past generations
See their work ended?
I tell myself it won't be that way
One day.

I tell myself I'm not clinging to hope
Give me time and it will all turn around
One day.
But what time do I have?
I don't have years
I don't have many months
But I have one day.
And I'll keep telling myself that
When I'm 49
I'll keep telling myself that
Always one day
I'll keep telling myself
Begging myself
Cajoling myself
Berating myself
Soothing myself
Fucking myself
And then telling myself
One day.

The Act Of Genevieve

A sunny evening, the shadows were long
Across the meadow, a green furlong
And all was calm and fair
A slight breeze wisped, a magpie chacked
A fallen tree from weather hacked
No human soul to care.

At length a sound of one to intrude
A scattering a small birds ensued
No less a song to call
Across the meadow a young woman strode
With the confidence of one's abode
A fading leaf to fall

The woman's name was Genevieve
A floral dress with a tufted sleeve
Lips of rouge and soft
She crossed a stile and walked on uphill
Sang a joyous song of a boundless will
Her arms were held aloft

At length she reached the churchyard gate
Will all to praise, none to berate
She entered, thus she graced
She wandered on and strode paths around

Then stopped at that which she had found
A new gravestone she faced

"Here Lies Thomas Anthony James
My Lord and Father, My Soul Reclaims"
The dates of thirty years
The second date a mere two years ago
The sign of a fate one does not know
To confound all wits and seers

For a year she had been Mr James's wife
He was handsome and cunning, sharp as a knife
Until he came to grief
How it had happened, no townsfolk knew
The superstition and rumours grew
With choice of one's belief

From her breast, a small phial Genevieve drew
From which fell liquid like mountain dew
And spattered on the soil
"More arsenic" she whispered, glancing low
The soil spat fumes, no grass to grow
No gain for Nature's toil

She turned and walked to the grave beside
A large stone furnished of scholarly pride
The motto no less bold
"Here Lies the Body of Septimus Jack
From Dust I Came, Now I Turn Back

Into My Saviour's Fold"

He was a teacher of the greatest repute
Firmness to render a magistrate mute
Retired and soon deceased
Genevieve herself had his tutelage known
For her learning the seeds were sown
And faculties increased

"More for you" she murmured with calm
The liquid fell, the soil to balm
And the she turned away
Her eyes betrayed an anger strong
Where wrath and fearful pride belong
But lips remained at play

She left the churchyard in the evening light
Blossoms were falling, pink and white
And nothing out of place
But pay heed now, her bare back reveals
The faint traces of old bruises and weals
That time does not erase

And so Genevieve walked and sang a hymn
To earthly bounty and Nature's whim
Her beauty shining on
And townsfolk talked and wondered yet
Of early passing and Maker met
Of lives that are now gone

The sun was fading, she crossed a field
The less the light of day to wield
And no more left to see
And time will pass with Nature's heart
All paths will cross and wind apart
While all the birds roam free.

Closure

Did you sense the sadness?
What did you learn?
Did you get my message?
Will you take your turn?

The hope hasn't gone yet
There's a prayer to be prayed
And I hope that you'll be there
As a future is made

But I don't keep my hopes up
I know where I stand
The odds are against me
Not at my command

Let this be my mission
Enjoy life while I may
For while I'm still here
There's still something to say

If I'm dead when you read this
Don't leave your life in vain
For it still has a purpose
And a love to retain

And if I'm still alive now
I thank you, my friend
Think of me as I go on
With a life to amend

Let us go our own ways now
And give thanks for our birth
Let our actions define us
Let our time be our worth.